W9-BOA-129

Religion in the public schools

shed by American Association of School Administrators, 1201 Sixteenth Street, N.W., Washington, D.C. 20036

.

RELIGION IN THE PUBLIC SCHOOLS

A report by the Commission on Religion in the Public
Schools, American Association of School Administrators

June 30, 1964

The Commission:

DONALD E. BOLES
Professor of Government
Iowa State University
Ames, Iowa

JOHN S. CARTWRIGHT
Professor of Education
Lehigh University
Bethlehem, Pennsylvania

DWIGHT L. KIRK
Superintendent of Schools
Odessa Public Schools
Odessa, Texas

JOHN HENRY MARTIN
Superintendent of Schools
Freeport Public Schools
Freeport, New York

THOMAS G. PULLEN, JR.
State Superintendent of Schools
Maryland State Department of Education
Baltimore, Maryland

SIDNEY P. MARLAND, JR., *CHAIRMAN*
Superintendent of Schools
Pittsburgh Public Schools
Pittsburgh, Pennsylvania

ARCHIBALD B. SHAW, *SECRETARY*
Associate Secretary
American Association of School Administrators
Washington, D.C.

ROLFE LANIER HUNT, *CONSULTANT*
Department of Church and Public School Relations
National Council of Churches of Christ in the U.S.A.
New York, N. Y.

TABLE OF CONTENTS

*"Religious freedom is . . . strongly imbedded
in our public and private life."*
*"Religion has been closely identified
with our history and government."*

INTRODUCTION

THE EXECUTIVE COMMITTEE of the American Association of
School Administrators charged this Commission to examine
the effect of recent decisions of the Supreme Court on the
issues of Bible reading and prayer in the public schools. The
charge further called upon us to suggest constructive means
by which public school administrators could guide the development of local policies and practices, responding to the
Court's interpretations of the Constitution on this subject.

The work of the Commission, accordingly, has been
limited to these topics, notwithstanding periodic temptations
to stray beyond the intended scope. For example, when one
speaks of religion and the public schools, one can easily drift
into consideration of several current topics not germane to
the charge: shared time, public funds for church-related
schools, released time, pupil transportation, etc. Crucial and
timely as these related issues are, they are dealt with here
only as they relate to the central concerns.

Semantic gymnastics could have led to discourse upon
the meaning of religion, excessive for the purposes of this
study. Indeed, recent Supreme Court decisions go so far as
to indicate by footnote that a religion does not necessarily
presuppose the existence of a Supreme Being. The Commission has declined to enter this arena, finding therein no useful
advantage in its present task. Religion has been treated, for
the purposes of this report, simply as an expression of creed

v

or practice of worship, organized or unorganized, denominationally labeled or not, systematic or not.

The members of the Commission represent a wide range of experience, denominational persuasions, and academic orientation. Representative religious views, including formal expressions by denominational bodies and informal by religious and philosophical leaders, as well as political and legal views, have been brought to bear in the deliberations. Where differences have occurred—and there have been many—we have threshed out the differences in council. No minority report or "dissenting opinion" has been necessary, although it was agreed at the start that such would be accommodated.

The burden of this message is the affirmative confrontation of the law concerning religious practices in public schools. It is the Commission's intent to provide a set of guidelines for those who frame local school policy and those who administer and teach within such policy.

No pretense is made that these guidelines are infallible. Some may be subject to Constitutional challenge now or in the future. The public schools of America, in their early days largely the creature of the churches, with strong religious orientation, are now directed by the First Amendment to disengage themselves wholly from churches and religious practices. At the same time the law cautions against hostility to religion. The narrow path between these admonitions is the route marked in the pages which follow.

The Commission has high hope that what may appear to some at this moment to be a regressive measure may indeed be a new forward thrust by education in its championship of freedom, including religious freedom. Not only is organized religion left undamaged by the Constitution as now read; the Commission, as a product of this inquiry, finds hope for a larger and deeper place for religion in our culture.

I

PUBLIC SCHOOLS AND THE HERITAGE
OF RELIGIOUS FREEDOM

THE FOUNDING FATHERS established for America a system of government that had existed before only in the minds of philosophers. Yet their work grew out of more than 150 years of a growing appetite for and experience in self-government in the colonies, and out of passionate convictions about the kind of civil government in which all men might be truly free. In the Preamble and in the first ten amendments (Bill of Rights) they built around the more prosaic structural description a series of statements of fundamental principles which forever defined the purposes and limited the powers of that government.

In the First Amendment they struck the boldest of blows for individual religious freedom and for a governmental

1

climate in which any and all religions or faiths might flourish. They created a seeming paradox in that double prohibition against any law respecting the establishment of religion and against any restriction on the free exercise of religion. This might have been interpreted as hostility to religion, yet its intent and its effects were exactly the reverse; hence the paradox. The great new bastion of freedom was erected in this amendment by men who recognized even then the essential pluralism of American society and the basic responsibility of a democratic government for the equal protection of all segments of that society, whatever their beliefs or lack of belief.

In the world of that era practically every nation, including the non-Christian, had an established religion. The resulting ills to the country and to the individual religionists were apparent to those who framed our own government. An established religion was a state religion with exclusive legal status, with some state controls over the church and individual, and with support from taxes laid by the state on all irrespective of their religious beliefs.

Many of the American colonies themselves had established churches. In those colonies dissenting sects such as Baptists, Roman Catholics, Quakers, and Jews were denied by law the right to assemble publicly and to worship. Individuals were heavily punished by fine, imprisonment, expulsion, and even in a few instances deaths for violations. The churches that were privileged by governmental establishment fought to preserve this privilege. Yet all the while the religiously oppressed cried out against the oppression and attacked the vested interests of the established church. Their resistance brought results.

The Commonwealth of Virginia, under the leadership of Thomas Jefferson, disestablished the Anglican church and laid the foundation for governmental neutrality in religion. Virginia, in its bill for religious freedom, provided that "to compel a man to furnish contributions of money for the propagation of opinions which he disbelieves and abhors, is sinful and tyrannical." This landmark legislation, adopted by a representative assembly, reflected the growing conviction that every man's religion was a very personal thing, to be held dearly. It said that his civil government had no business forcing him to conform to any set of religious beliefs or to support a particular religious body.

In the main the founding fathers were religious men, affiliated with one of the several sects then found in the colonies. Had they been irreligious or had they desired to make the country irreligious, they might have anticipated the official atheism of the French Revolution of their day. Significantly they did not. They proclaimed in the First Amendment their faith that people of all denominations, and of none, should get along together and that all religions could prosper best when the commonwealth gave no preferment to any and made of none a state religion.

One basis for prohibiting the establishment of religion in America was and continues to be the great diversity of religious beliefs and religious institutions. Every religion can be protected only as it supports that protection for all other religions and for nonbelievers as well. The individual's responsibility is as fully clear. This is another expression of the doctrine that the safety of a democracy rests upon vigilance toward those in authority and not upon the good intentions and benevolence of individuals, lest there arise a Pharaoh that "knew not Joseph."

Over the years under the benign neutrality of our federal government and states, religious institutions have grown and prospered. Individuals have come to be free to worship or

3

not as they desire, without persecution. As the people have become better educated and more closely involved in government the right of every individual not to be penalized under law because of his religion has gained general acceptance. The growing pluralism of our society has strengthened this view. Philosophically, complete adherence to this concept of neutrality means not a denial of religion but rather a recognition of the religious integrity of each individual. It means that the public schools carry a high obligation to ensure the individual freedoms essential to this goal.

The Commission therefore accepts and supports the decisions of the Supreme Court respecting prayer and Bible reading in the public schools of the nation. The Commission agrees with the Supreme Court when it stated further: "Religion has been closely identified with our history and government. This is not to say, however, that religion has been so identified with our history and government that religious freedom is not likewise as strongly imbedded in our public and private life."

This is the setting and the charge to the public schools. It poses dilemmas which your Commission endeavors to confront.

Public schools are indispensable to American democracy. Their chief responsibility is to develop moral and literate citizens for the general and individual good. Along with government and all its agencies, the schools must be neutral in respect to the religious beliefs of individual citizens. But this does not mean in any sense that public schools are or should be irreligious. To say that public schools are irreligious, merely because they do not follow the prescribed prayer of a religious segment of the population or because they do not recognize officially the distinctive practices or creed of any religious segment, is to say that government itself is irreligious

4

or even antireligious. This is not true. There is no threat to the individual, to religion, or to the common good in the removal of religious exercises from the schools.

Public schools bring together individuals irrespective of race, creed, color, or wealth in their student body and faculty. They include more Catholic children than all the Catholic schools at every level combined; they include more Jewish children than all the Jewish schools combined; they include more Protestant children than all the Protestant schools combined; and they include more children of free thinkers than all the schools operated by people of these viewpoints combined. The public schools include in their enrollment the children of all races. Indeed the public schools are a meeting-ground and focus of America's pluralism.

The public schools are probably the most religiously tolerant of all institutions in our democracy. There is some evidence to show that the children who attend public schools are as religious and moral as children who attend nonpublic schools. In the selection of their teachers the public schools manifest a belief in the power of education in the search for truth and in the cooperation of people of all religious beliefs working together for the improvement of mankind. They are an expression of brotherhood in the diversity of the children they enroll and the teachers they employ. Recognizing that a teacher's religious beliefs do not necessarily distort his conception of the truth, the public schools demonstrate a faith in educational objectivity and a respect for all religions and for religion in general.

The practices that the Supreme Court found incompatible with the First Amendment were by no means universal. A number of state constitutions have long expressly forbidden the use of the Bible and prayer or religious worship in the public schools. In other states many schools have

5

squarely faced some of the questions now raised nationally by the Supreme Court decisions. In some, questions have been raised about the use of books that are offensive to children of various religious faiths. Questions have arisen about certain programs of a religious nature in the schools. The teaching of some historical events has aroused controversy on religious grounds. The field of possible conflict and concern is broad indeed, yet the public schools are slowly moving to reconcile their practices with the magnificent ideal so firmly set out in the First Amendment.

There is a very fine line between teaching, impersonally and objectively, facts about events, individuals, and institutions of a religious nature that have affected history and contemporary life and advocating in that teaching a specific point of view. Many teachers, exercising common sense and good manners and themselves broadly educated, have proved they can handle this delicate task with propriety, fairness, and objectivity.

The members of the Commission, from their experience as school administrators, assert their confidence in the integrity and the growing competence of teachers to fulfill this mission. With this confidence they have a well-founded faith that under the Constitution, with its unfolding interpretation, the public schools can continue to embody and foster the great American dream of liberty and justice for all.

II

THE LAW: ITS BASIS
AND ITS IMPLICATIONS

THE CONSTITUTION means what the Supreme Court says it means—it's as simple as that. This principle is a fundamental characteristic of government by law in our democratic society. The public schools have a special responsibility to guard and transmit our governmental heritage to the oncoming generations. That responsibility carries with it three clearly defined obligations:

1. To support and defend the Constitution, as so many have so often sworn themselves to do;

2. To understand and teach what loyalty to the United States and support for its constitutional form of government involves in citizen rights and duties;

3. To distinguish clearly between the citizen's obligation to obey existing law on the one hand, and his inherent right to seek to repeal or amend law through due process on the other.

* Public school leaders share with all other governmental officials the obligation to understand and obey the law at every level. In addition, they are entrusted uniquely with the task of transmitting their commitment to the American constitutional form of government by example, practice, and education to the children and youth of America.

The Commission properly assumes that school administrators themselves give full allegiance and prompt obedience to the law, notwithstanding the fact that many leaders in politics, in the press, and even in religious bodies may appear to advocate defiance of the law. Equally, it confidently assumes that they need no support or enlightenment in the processes constitutionally open to all citizens in expressing opposition to and effecting change in the Constitution.

In this section the Commission undertakes a practical analysis of what the Supreme Court has said about the religion clauses in the First Amendment as applied to the public schools. Its purpose is to provide a working guide to present constitutional provisions for the benefit of practitioners in public school administration.

The First Amendment to the United States Constitution provides that "Congress shall make no law respecting an establishment of religion, or prohibiting the free exercise thereof. . . ." The American Constitution in this respect is unique among those of most countries in the free world since not only do we have freedom of religion assured, but government is prohibited from establishing a religion. The United States thus differs from Great Britain, for example, in that although the latter nation allows its people "freedom of religion," at the same time it maintains a single established church.

It is crucial to an understanding of the Constitution to understand the intent of its framers. When there is disagreement or debate on what the Constitution means, however, the final determination rests with the Supreme Court. This truism applies to the religion clauses of the First Amendment. Thus to know what practices with religious overtones are permitted or prohibited in the public schools it is necessary to analyze key decisions of the Supreme Court. In doing so, it is important to recognize dangers in attempting to expand court doctrine beyond the specific issues raised in each case. While it is normal, and sometimes necessary, to attempt educated guesses as to how specific decisions might be applied to peripheral problem areas, it must be understood that the decisions themselves must come from the Supreme Court.

The First Amendment—Freedom of Religion

No right was more crucial to the early history of the United States than religious freedom. It was the pursuit of this liberty that brought many of the early colonists to the New World, even though in many instances they were unwilling to guarantee religious liberty to all in the colonies they established here. Indeed, religious persecution in early American history helps explain why in the Bill of Rights the first clauses of the First Amendment provide "Congress shall make no law respecting an establishment of religion, or prohibiting the free exercise thereof. . . ."

It is worth noting that while religious controversies of one sort or another are rather common in American history, until recently relatively few have been brought to the Supreme Court for solution. The great bulk of court law on

9

the subject of the First Amendment provisions on religion has developed since 1940. Indeed, it is not until the 1960's that some of the more crucial issues in this field have been ruled on by the Supreme Court.

Freedom of Religion

The Supreme Court has in general had less difficulty in defining and applying the "freedom of religion" clause than it has with the clause dealing with the "establishment of religion." Concerning the freedom of religion, the Court has devised a frame of reference which views such freedom on three different levels—the right to *believe*, the right to *advocate* religious beliefs, and the right to *practice* one's religious beliefs. The degree of protection a person receives will vary on each level, the Court has made clear.

For example, the right to *believe* is absolute and cannot be abridged. To the present, every person has always been held to be secure in the privacy of his own thoughts and beliefs.

While relatively unrestrained, the right to *advocate* one's religious beliefs can be curtailed, according to the Supreme Court, if there is immediate danger of substantial injury to others. It is not enough for such advocacy merely to injure others, it must result in substantial injury. For example, the Court might accept a regulation prohibiting religious advocacy which appears to incite the violent elimination of members of other religious sects.

In viewing the right to *practice* one's religion it is clear that less freedom is authorized by the Court for the practice of religion than there is for the right to advocate religion and certainly much less than is permitted for the right to believe. This distinction was made clear in the so-called Mormon

10

Cases in the 1880's, some of the earliest cases to come before the Court dealing with the freedom of religion. In *Reynolds v. U.S.* (1879), certain Mormons challenged the constitutionality of the federal statute governing the territory of Utah which made bigamy a crime. They alleged that this law violated the freedom of religion guaranteed by the First Amendment, since a basic tenet of the Mormon faith was a belief in plural marriages.

The Supreme Court ruled that the free exercise of religion guaranteed in the First Amendment is an absolute right only with respect to beliefs. The Congress could, however, as a valid exercise of its duty to protect the health, welfare, and morals of the nation, impose reasonable regulations which might have the effect of restraining certain religious practices. In essence what the Court said was that while the Mormons could believe that they could or should have plural marriages, they simply could not practice these beliefs in this country. More recently, the same judicial reasoning was used to reject the charges by certain Southern religious groups, who handled poisonous snakes during religious services, that state laws outlawing these practices violated the freedom of religion.

In the 1960's the Supreme Court was confronted with the charge that Sunday closing laws—sometimes called Blue Laws—violated the freedom of religion guaranteed by the First Amendment (for example: *McGowan v. Maryland*, 1961). These state laws, which made it a crime to conduct business activities on a Sunday, were held by the Court not to violate the Constitution, but on rather specific grounds. While such laws may have originally been enacted to force people to attend church, the Court held that this was no longer their intent. The contemporary purpose behind laws of this type was secular rather than religious, and their intent was to designate one day for rest, relaxation, and family companionship.

The modern Supreme Court has tended to follow a case-to-case approach in clarifying the concept of religious freedom. An example of this can be seen in its decision, also in 1961, which declared unconstitutional a Maryland law requiring a profession in the belief in the existence of God before one could hold public office.

In a similar vein, the Supreme Court in 1943 overruled its decision of three years earlier and declared that a state could not force public school students to salute the flag if the students in good faith felt such a practice violated their religious beliefs. Such governmental action violated the freedom of religion clause of the First Amendment, the Court explained. *(West Virginia Board of Education v. Barnette,* 1943; overruling *Minersville School District v. Gobitis,* 1940.)

In 1952, the Supreme Court was confronted with an important case revealing the close relationship between freedom of religion and freedom of speech and press. In *Burstyn v. Wilson,* the Court held unconstitutional a New York State statute which authorized the state to refuse to permit the showing of any moving picture films which were found to be "obscene, indecent, immoral, inhuman, (or) sacrilegious. . . ." Although the Court's decision is felt by some to be ambiguous as to whether the statute violated freedom of religion, freedom of press, or both, Justice Clark speaking for the Court made it clear that a state could not censor films because they might be sacrilegious. If this were permitted it would in reality require the state to determine what is religion in order to judge what is sacrilegious. The Court noted that "the state has no legitimate interest in protecting any or all religions from views distasteful to them which is sufficient to justify prior restraint upon the expression of these views."

The Establishment of Religion

The Supreme Court has frequently suggested that different rights are protected by the "freedom of religion" clause of the First Amendment and the "establishment of religion" clause. The distinction may be seen by noting the situation in England or Burma where religious freedom has been assured but there has been an established church in both nations. Nonetheless as a practical matter it is frequently difficult to draw a line in a specific case between issues of religious freedom or those involving the establishment of religion.

The Everson Case

Probably no case better demonstrates this point than the significant case of *Everson v. the Board of Education* decided by the Supreme Court in 1947. The *Everson* case, arising in New Jersey, is important since it may be seen as the opening salvo in the contemporary battle over governmental aid to parochial schools. It also indicated a trend to use the schools as the primary arena in which to fight the battle over what constitutes an "establishment" of religion.

The facts in the case are relatively simple. A state statute of New Jersey permitted the use of public funds to pay for the bus transportation of parochial school students to parochial school. One school district in the state adopted a regulation authorizing public funds to be paid to transport Roman Catholic parochial school students to Roman Catholic parochial schools. The local regulation and state statute were challenged on the grounds that they violated the First Amendment's provisions prohibiting an establishment of religion and denying the free exercise of religion.

Speaking for a majority of the Supreme Court in a 5 to 4 decision Justice Black emphasized that the First Amendment created a wall of separation between church and state. This wall was to be high and impregnable, he explained, and could not be breached in the slightest. The First Amendment prohibited governmental aid or assistance to any and all religions. The Court said: "Neither the state nor the Federal Government can set up a church. Neither can pass laws that aid one religion, aid all religions or prefer one religion over another. Neither can force nor influence a person to go to or to remain away from church . . . or force him to profess a belief or disbelief in any religion. . . . No tax in any amount, large or small, can be levied to support any religious activities or institutions, whatever they may be called, or whatever form they may adopt to teach or practice religion. Neither a state nor the Federal Government can, openly or secretly, participate in the affairs of any religious organization or groups or vice versa. In the words of Jefferson, the clause against establishment of religion by law was intended to erect a wall of separation between church and state."

Despite this emphasis, however, the majority of the Court concluded that providing public funds for Roman Catholic school bus transportation was not aid to religion. It was, said Justice Black, aid to the students. Such a program did not violate the First Amendment since it was designed to promote the welfare of the child, not to aid or establish a religion.

Justice Jackson, one of the four dissenting Justices in the *Everson* case, registered shock at the conclusion. The majority opinion reminded him, he said, of Donna Julia, in Lord Byron's poem *Don Juan*. That lady, "while crying she would ne'er consent, consented," Justice Jackson observed.

It is important to remember, however, that the *Everson* case did not make it compulsory for a state to provide aid for parochial school bus transportation. It merely stated that the

14

First Amendment does not prohibit such a practice if a state's constitution and laws permit assistance of this type.

The McCollum *Case*

The *McCollum* case, decided by the Supreme Court in 1948, is one of the most important decisions in the field of religion and the schools. It involved a practice common to many public schools of the United States then—that of "released time." As practiced by such schools released time programs involved setting aside a portion of the school day, during regular class hours, in which representatives of various religious sects would use school classrooms to instruct students of their faith in the principle of that sect. Students were not compelled to attend, but those who did not participate were compelled to pursue their regular secular studies in the school study hall.

Mrs. McCollum brought a mandamus suit to prevent the continuation of a released time program in the public schools of Champaign, Illinois. She alleged such programs constituted a use of public funds for sectarian purposes in violation of the Illinois Constitution and laws and also constituted a denial of the equal protection of the laws guaranteed by the Fourteenth Amendment to the United States Constitution. But more important she contended that these programs violated the establishment and freedom of religion clauses of the First Amendment.

The Supreme Court by an 8 to 1 vote declared these programs to be unconstitutional. Speaking for the majority, Justice Black rejected the argument that the First Amendment was intended to forbid only governmental preference to one religion over another, but not impartial governmental assistance to all religions. He went on to explain that the First

Amendment "rests upon the premise that both religion and government can best achieve their lofty aims if each is left free from the other within its respective sphere."

Justice Black concluded: "Here not only are the state's tax-supported public school buildings used for the dissemination of religious doctrines. The state also affords sectarian groups an invaluable aid in that it helps to provide pupils for the religious classes through use of the state's compulsory public school machinery. This is not separation of church and state."

An important feature about this opinion is the unwillingness of four Justices in the majority sweepingly to declare illegal all forms and varieties of religious programs similar in any way to the Champaign plan. Justice Frankfurter made it clear that the Court was dealing with one plan of "released time" and left the door open for a different decision regarding other types of programs. He explained: "We do not consider, as indeed we could not, school programs not before us which though colloquially characterized as 'released time' present situations differing in aspects which may well be constitutionally crucial."

The Zorach *Case*

The *McCollum* decision received a highly mixed reaction from religious groups in the nation. Roman Catholics were especially disturbed over it. Protestant Evangelicals were disappointed. The decision was praised, however, by the *Christian Century,* by Unitarians, Baptists, and most Jewish groups. Nonetheless, it was a most controversial decision. This is important to keep in mind to help one understand the seemingly paradoxical ruling in the *Zorach* case four years later.

The fact situation in the *Zorach* case involved a religious instruction program similar to that in the *McCollum* case, the major difference being that instead of utilizing public school classrooms, the program of instruction was given off school property at various religious centers. The programs were, however, conducted during regular school hours during the school day. Students were not compelled to attend, but if they did not they were required to stay in their classrooms.

This program was challenged on the grounds that it violated the establishment of religion provision of the First Amendment. In 1952, by a 6 to 3 vote, the Supreme Court ruled that the program had neither prohibited the free exercise of religion nor constituted a law "respecting an establishment of religion." Speaking for the majority, Justice Douglas felt that "it takes obtuse reasoning to inject any issue of 'free exercise' of religion into the present case."

"The First Amendment," Douglas noted, "does not say that in every and all respects there shall be a separation of Church and State." If that were the case, Justice Douglas believed churches could not be required to pay property taxes nor could police or fire protection be provided by municipalities to churches. "A fastidious atheist or agnostic," Douglas noted, "could even object to the supplication with which the Court opens each session, 'God save the United States and this Honorable Court.' " This comment is worth remembering in connection with Justice Douglas' concurring opinion, in a later case, holding unconstitutional nonsectarian prayers in the public schools.

In *Zorach,* Justice Douglas said: "We are a religious people whose institutions presuppose a Supreme Being." The Court went on to explain that while the First Amendment forbade government financing of religious groups and of religious instruction, the Amendment did not require govern-

17

mental hostility to religion. While the Court could find no evidences in the specific case of public coercion to force public school students into the programs complained of, it held that if evidence of coercion existed, a wholly different case would be presented.

The dissenters felt that school facilities were being used here just as in the *McCollum* case, since regular school hours were being used for religious exercises. Justice Frankfurter noted:

> *There is all the difference in the world between letting the children out of school and letting some out of school into religious classes. . . . The pith of the case is that formalized religious instruction is substituted for other school activities which those who do not participate in the released time program are compelled to attend.*

Justice Jackson, in dissenting, pointed out that the greater effectiveness of this system over a strictly voluntary program of religious instruction taking place after school hours "is due to the truant officer who, if the youngster fails to go to the church school, dogs him back to the public school room." Thus the school "serves as a temporary jail for the student who will not go to church," Jackson explained.

How does one square the rule of the *McCollum* case with that of *Zorach?* At a minimum, it seems safe to generalize in the following fashion. The First and Fourteenth Amendments are violated if the public schools release students from classes to attend religious exercises in the school building. On the other hand, it is legal for the public schools to dismiss their charges from classes to attend religious instruction outside of the public school property so long as school officials in no way attempt to coerce students to attend the religious programs.

18

The Engel *Case*

In 1962, the Supreme Court, in a decision of major importance, by a vote of 6 to 1 struck down a state-sponsored optional program of nondenominational prayer in the public schools of New York State. Acting upon a recommendation of the State Board of Regents, the New Hyde Park Board of Education had directed the school district's principal to cause all teachers to open each school day with the following prayer: "Almighty God, we acknowledge our dependence upon Thee, and we beg Thy blessings upon us, our parents, our teachers and our country."

Speaking for the majority, Justice Black from the outset left no doubt that the New York practice was wholly inconsistent with the establishment clause of the First Amendment. By its very nature prayer is religious, and the Constitutional prohibition against establishing a religion must at a minimum mean that in the United States "it is no part of the business of government to compose official prayers for any group of the American people to recite as a part of a religious program carried on by government," Black explained. Noting the historical reasons for including the establishment clause in the Bill of Rights, Black pointed out that Americans of that day "knew the anguish, hardship and bitter strife that could come when zealous religious groups struggled with one another to obtain the Government's stamp of approval." The First Amendment stands as a guarantee that "the people's religion must not be subjected to the pressures of government for change each time a new political administration is elected to office," Justice Black noted.

The Court rejected the argument that its holding would be construed as indicating a hostility to religion or to prayer. "Nothing . . . could be more wrong," the Court insisted, for

19

the "history of man is inseparable from the history of religion." Neither were the founding fathers hostile to religion or prayer. They drafted the First Amendment to "quiet well-justified fears . . . arising out of an awareness that governments in the past had shackled men's tongues to make them speak only the religious thoughts that government wanted them to speak and to pray only to the God that government wanted them to pray to," the Court explained.

The Court made it clear, however, that nothing in the decision should be construed as discouraging school children from reciting historical documents such as the Declaration of Independence, containing references to the Deity, or singing "officially espoused anthems" which contain the composer's profession of faith in a Supreme Being. "Such patriotic or ceremonial occasions," the Court insisted, "bear no true resemblance to the unquestioned religious exercise that the state of New York has sponsored. . . ."

The majority opinion rests primarily on the general base that an official governmental enactment requiring or permitting a specific religious practice violates the Establishment Clause. Government on any level in the United States, the Court felt, has no business legislating on matters of religion. It is immaterial whether or not such governmental programs require an expenditure of public funds.

The concurring opinion of Justice Douglas here is interesting in light of his position in the *Zorach* case and the *Everson* case. "What New York does at the opening of its public schools," Douglas observed, "is what we do when we open court." The Supreme Court is convened by its marshal with the saying "God save the United States and this Honorable Court." Moreover, Congress opens each day with its chaplains asking for divine guidance for the Congressmen.

20

The situation involving New York teachers, the marshal of the Supreme Court, and the Congressional chaplains have one thing in common—they are all on the public payroll. While the amounts of public money involved in each of these programs are minuscule, Douglas noted, each situation involves a public official on a public payroll performing a religious exercise in a governmental institution. An element of coercion in such programs was detected by Justice Douglas since "few adults, let alone children, would leave our Courtroom or the Senate or the House while those prayers are being given. Every such audience is in a sense a 'captive' audience." Douglas explained also that "once government finances a religious exercise it inserts a divisive influence into our communities."

In a passage which constitutional lawyers noted with special interest, Justice Douglas commented:

> *My problem today would be uncomplicated but for* Everson v. Board of Education . . . *which allowed taxpayers' money to be used to pay "the bus fares of parochial school pupils." . . . The* Everson *case seems in retrospect to be out of line with the First Amendment. Its result is appealing, as it allows aid to be given to needy children. Yet by the same token, public funds could be used to satisfy other needs of children in parochial schools—lunches, books, and tuition being obvious examples.*

It is clear that Justice Douglas has reversed his position from that of the *Everson* case. If Justice Black, who wrote the majority opinion in both the *Everson* case and the *Engel* case, agreed with Douglas on this change in viewpoint, he did not make it explicit in the latter opinion. Justice Black is the only other member of the Court originally hearing the *Everson* appeal who is still on the bench. Seven new Justices have joined the Court since that decision. If a similar question were to be brought before the Court as now constituted, there is no certainty as to whether the Court would reach the same conclusions as in the *Everson* case.

The Schempp *Case*

In 1963 the Supreme Court faced up to one of the most commonly found religiously-oriented programs in public schools—that of Bible-reading exercises. While two cases arising in two different states—Pennsylvania and Maryland —were involved, because of the similarity in state laws and the fact situation the Supreme Court treated them as one case. The Pennsylvania statute which serves as a focus of the case required that:

> *At least ten verses of the Holy Bible shall be read, without comment, at the opening of each public school on each school day. Any child shall be excused from such Bible reading, upon the written request of his parent or guardian.*

By an 8 to 1 vote, the Supreme Court held such laws and practices violated the establishment clause of the First Amendment as applied to the states by the Fourteenth Amendment. Speaking for the majority, Justice Clark noted that "religion has been closely identified with our history and government." He went on to explain: "This is not to say, however, that religion has been so identified with our history and government that religious freedom is not likewise as strongly embedded in our public and private life." The Court emphasized the importance of freedom of worship especially to a nation which is composed of citizens drawn from the four corners of the world and in which 83 separate religious bodies, each with over 50,000 members, function.

22

In addition there are, of course, innumerable smaller religious sects functioning in the United States.

The Court rejected "unequivocally" the contention that the establishment clause forbids "only government preference of one religion over another." Quoting Justice Rutledge in an earlier opinion, the Court explained that:

> *The [First] Amendment's purpose was not to strike merely at the official establishment of a single...religion. .... It was to create a complete and permanent separation of the spheres of religious activity and civil authority by comprehensively forbidding every form of public aid or support for religion.*

Justice Clark emphasized the First Amendment's requirement that the government remain neutral to religion, in the following words:

> *This wholesome "neutrality"... stems from a recognition of the teachings of history that powerful sects or groups might bring about a fusion of governmental and religious functions ... to the end that official support of ... Government would be placed behind the tenets of one or of all orthodoxies.*

The Court then fashioned a test to determine if a state law or practice violated the establishment clause. The test as the Court saw it was: "What are the purposes and primary effect of the enactment?" The First Amendment is violated, the Court announced, "if either [the purpose or primary effect of the law] is the advancement or inhibition of religion." To clarify this position the Court emphasized again that there was a distinction between the establishment clause and the free exercise clause, and a given action might violate one but not the other. "A violation of the Free Exercise Clause is predicated on coercion while the Establishment Clause need not be so attended," Justice Clark explained.

The programs attacked in these cases are prescribed as part of the curricular activities of students who are required by law to attend school. Moreover, the religious character of the exercise was admitted by the state, the Court explained, since the alternate use of denominational versions of the Bible was permitted. This does not square, therefore, with the states' contention that the Bible was used either as an "instrument for non-religious moral inspiration, or as a reference for the teaching of secular subjects," Justice Clark observed.

"It is no defense," the Court noted, "to urge that the religious practices here may be relatively minor encroachments on the First Amendment. The breach of neutrality that is today a trickling stream may all too soon become a raging torrent." Quoting Madison, the Court emphasized "it is proper to take alarm at the first experiment on our liberties."

Justice Clark denied that this decision would establish a "religion of secularism" in the schools. He went on to say that "one's education is not complete without a study of comparative religion or the history of religion." Moreover, the Court saw the study of the literary and historic qualities of the Bible as worthy.

Finally the Court rejected the argument that to prohibit a religious exercise approved by the majority would collide with the majority's right to free exercise of religion. The clause "has never meant that a majority could use the machinery of the state to practice its beliefs." The Court felt that Justice Jackson in an earlier opinion effectively answered that contention. Jackson explained:

> *The very purpose of a Bill of Rights was to withdraw certain subjects from the vicissitudes of political con-*

24

*troversy, to place them beyond the reach of majorities.
. . . One's right to . . . freedom of worship . . . and other
fundamental rights may not be submitted to vote, they
depend on the outcome of no elections.*

In summary the Court's opinion makes it clear that religious exercises of this sort need not be compulsory for students in order for the practice to violate the establishment
clause. Nor must they involve substantial expenditures of
public funds to fail the test of constitutionality.

Conclusion

The Court has by no means dealt with every issue that
may arise or every public school practice with a religious
implication. There are still large gray areas in which the
principal guidance to date may be the tests of "purpose and
primary effect," in the words of the decision in the *Schempp*
case. If the purpose or primary effect of a practice is the
"advancement or inhibition of religion," then the Court seems
to say that it is unconstitutional for the government, and
hence the public schools, to require or support such a practice.

At the same time the public schools are clearly enjoined
from hostility to religion, and their essential neutrality may
not be construed as support for antireligion or justification
for the preferment of a nonreligious philosophy.

The Court's definition of religion itself is not entirely
clear. Throughout most of the Court's decisions it has seemed
to involve expressions of religious faith and reliance upon a
Supreme Being, and to be tested in part by affiliation with
one or more institutions of fellow-believers referred to as
churches. Yet in 1962, in striking down a state's requirement
that an officeholder swear to his belief in God, the Court
seemed to hold that a nontheistic philosophy which serves

as a controlling ideal in a person's life falls properly under the protection of the First Amendment.

Finally, the Commission especially notes, in the words of Justice Jackson, that this is a subject of "magnitude, intricacy and delicacy." The work of the Commission in the controversial areas in public school practice and policy has been undertaken not only in the spirit of full acceptance of the law but equally in awareness of those very qualities of its task. The guidelines and recommendations in subsequent sections of its report must be read accordingly.

III

CONSTRUCTIVE POLICIES
FOR PUBLIC SCHOOLS

THE RECENT SUPREME COURT DECISIONS on prayer and Bible reading alarmed many people. At first impact the rulings seemed to be both restrictive and negative. In fact public school practices and policies initially were affected most by the prohibition of certain practices. This naturally led to a presumption of loss.

But after the first reaction, the constructive possibilities began to be recognized. The positive effects of the decisions were to stimulate some rigorous thinking about public education in general, and specifically about the assumptions that important values were being developed and sustained by the daily ritual of Bible reading and prayer—an assumption that needed critical examination. To the extent that people everywhere, both in school and out, have been led to re-examine both their practices and their assumptions in the matters at issue, the decision has been clearly constructive.

Implicit in our system of government is the principle that no one religion or group of religions may dominate, but all must honor the religious convictions and practices of others. To tolerate is not enough. Honoring our differences means making room for them. It means understanding and valuing people for their differences, not merely focusing on surface similarities. It gives support to a genuinely intercultural education—one which strengthens mutual understanding and respect. In the long run, informed respect will strengthen the individual cultures themselves.

The public schools, as agencies of civil government, must be neutral with respect to the claims of the many religions and philosophies to the devotion and faith of their followers. At the same time they are charged, along with the civil government itself, with the responsibility to provide an environment in which practices and values that are rooted in the homes and churches can flourish. It is in response to this double duty that school policies that are truly constructive must be formulated.

The Commission proposes that constructive policy must be developed in every school district that will not only guarantee freedom from the establishment of religion but equally will foster freedom for religion. In the two chapters that follow it examines a number of areas and issues which call for such policy.

The observance of Christmas in public schools is one such area of issue. Because observance is so nearly universal, and because it so well illustrates the problems and complexities involved in establishing sound policy, the Commission discusses it first, in the pages that follow.

28

The report deals next with policies affecting the school calendar. It proposes that a constructive policy does not penalize or make unduly difficult but rather encourages the fulfillment of the individual's religious obligations on the part of any of the schools' people, student or staff. Beside the calendar itself, other accommodations may be required in personnel policies, examination schedules, and the like.

Continuing, the Commission turns to the schools' out-of-school demands and after-school activities, proposing that they should reflect a concern for the proper claims of other youth-serving agencies and of home and church on the time and loyalty of children.

In another area the Commission suggests that a study of the composition of the schools' staff may be relevant. It points out advantages that may accrue in better communication, as well as those that are inherent educationally, when a staff embodies the religious pluralism that is so characteristic of the society in which the school children will work and live.

Finally in Chapter IV, the Commission examines such practices as baccalaureates, dedications, and invocations, and reaches some policy recommendations that accommodate to religious pluralism yet are consistent with the traditional bases for the ceremonials.

In Chapter V, the Commission turns to an examination of some of the affirmative obligations of the schools in dealing with religion. It calls attention to three areas in the school's curriculum which require careful formulation of policy and sound development of materials and practice.

One difficult area is the recognition to be given to religion in the curriculum. In the Commission's judgment, constructive policy requires that the curriculum will actively recognize the impact of religion, both institutional and individual, and of religiously based ideas and ideals as forces

29

which have affected man's life as recorded in history, literature, and art.

The second area discussed by the Commission is the development and maintenance of values in the school's curriculum, organization, and activities. Here it is proposed that sound educational and public policy will honor the accumulated wisdom that supports the necessity and value of every individual's commitment to something higher than self and more than the passing moment.

Finally, the Commission proposes that the public school, as carrier and interpreter of the national heritage, must build in its young people an understanding of the great purposes of our Constitution, particularly its clauses on the establishment of religion and the free exercise of religion. At the minimum the schools must produce enlightened citizens who will be able to trace the probable long consequences of any alternative policies of government.

In the pages that follow the Commission assumes no special competence to prescribe. However, it has tried to analyze the issues and to examine critically a number of school policies and practices which may have bearing. Wherever possible it has recommended the policy or practice among those it has studied that it regards as most constructive and most consistent with Constitutional principles.

IV

ACCOMMODATIONS
TO RELIGIOUS PLURALISM

A. Constructive Policies for Christmas in the Schools

AFTER BIBLE READING AND PRAYER, no other exercise or occasion in the public schools provides so much difficulty for those who recognize that even a multidenominational religion may not be "established" than does Christmas.

Christmas has come to be a joyous and festive season in America. At the same time in the commercial world it is now the big selling season. Carols are sung in banks and railroad stations. Public address systems ring out with Christmas music. Long before December first, shopping centers and main streets are decorated, and bells jingle on every down-

31

town corner. Radio and television programs going out over the nonsectarian ether build up to the big day. Village greens, commons, and squares are aglow with Christmas trees and lights. Half the nation follows breathlessly the erection and lighting of the huge tree at Rockefeller Plaza, or the municipal tree downtown. The "national" tree in Washington blazes at the touch of the President's finger on the button. Christmas is everywhere.

Yet two sets of voices are increasingly being raised in protest. Some Christian religious leaders passionately protest the growing commercialization and secularization of the Advent. Christmas, they remind us, is a religious event, a true holy day which celebrates the birth of Him whose name it bears and whom they serve. They fear that this central fact gets blurred and diffused in the secular customs with which the day has become encrusted.

Another group speaks for the millions of Americans of different religions or philosophies. They protest the all-pervasive Christmas. They do not begrudge their Christian brothers' celebrations, but do protest the air of official support inherent in the use of governmental funds and agencies in the celebrations. They want to protect their young people from growing to feel that they are second-class citizens in a country which, professing no establishment of religion, seems in fact annually to endorse and support one. Particularly are they sensitive to the atmosphere and activities in the public schools which are their children's principal contact with government, and in which they learn by precept and practice the rights and responsibilities of citizenship.

A third group, in many American communities the largest one, likes things as they are. They are especially sensitive to any possibility of change in those public schools in which Christmas customs have grown almost into tradition. They come from no single denomination. Their own beliefs are diverse. Yet they have in common a concern lest something be lost in the change.

It is hard to arrive at a resolution of the problems at any time, and usually almost impossible in the Christmas season itself. But calm reflection away from the almost-frenzy of the Christmas season may lead to a better understanding of the dangers as seen by both the protesting groups and the protectors of local tradition. At other seasons it is easier to think as citizens, to re-examine our Constitutional compact, to understand again why it is that in America we can not have an establishment of religion—even of a sort of vaguely nondenominational Christianity.

There have not been many cases in our courts which bear specifically on Christmas celebrations in the public schools, although the basic law does seem clear. Under the Constitution, the public schools may not sponsor a religious service or service of worship, whether it be for a single or multidenominational group. Neither may public schools support or promote the Christian religions, Christian churches, nor distinctively Christian doctrines either exclusively or along with other religions, churches, and their distinctive doctrines.

In nearly all school districts, the following four generalizations seem warranted, and must be considered in making policy.

1. By long custom and nearly universal practice, the Christmas season has a special significance both in community custom and folk culture. The schools may not without violating the principles of learning ignore this element in the children's environment. Further, in drama, music, and art there is a very large body of works related to the Christmas theme and season that have entered into the Western world's culture.

33

2. Many Christian religious leaders deplore strongly the modern tendency "to take the Christ out of Christmas" and hence oppose secularized and nonreligious observances of one of Christianity's holiest days, whether in the public schools or elsewhere.

3. The celebration of the birth of Christ is almost unique in the degree to which it is shared by enrolled members of every Christian denomination and by many without formal church affiliations. It enlists a larger majority of our citizens and touches individuals and families in that majority more centrally than does any other holy day.

4. Public school teachers and administrators are by their profession sensitive to the needs and interests of children in society, and by their office responsible for understanding and supporting the laws of the land. In Christmas they are faced with an occasion that is based on doctrinal religion, which many of them hold deeply. It is strongly charged emotionally with tenderness towards children, which they share especially. It is not covered specifically and in detail by clear-cut guides. And it is encrusted with tradition and reinforced by widespread governmental example (White House Christmas Tree, for one) to support that tradition.

In the light of these generalizations, the issues can be narrowed somewhat. A public school, whatever the feelings of its constituents, may not observe Christmas as though it were a church or combination of churches. On the other hand an educational institution for children may not, consistent with proven educational principles of readiness and interest, ignore Christmas. Finally, the good public school will be highly sensitive to its obligation to support and protect the religious development of every child in its charge, in whatever religious tradition he and his family embrace. In this last may be found the key to sound policy.

The non-Christian is not a guest in a Christian school—he is a fellow citizen in a public school which includes a good many Christian members. His customs and beliefs are not shared by as many of his fellows as share the Christian traditions, usually, but he finds the public school a place and school teachers and administrators the kind of people who welcome him for himself, whatever his beliefs or his family's faith. He grows in love and respect for a school and a governmental system which cherish diversity, including religious diversity, while it supports each member's faith and belief without preferment. The message of peace on earth and good will among men is given real meaning.

At school the child will sing more songs from the Christian heritage—not as a worshiper, of course—because there *are* more and he joins the others in wanting to share them. But some of the music will be in his own religious tradition on appropriate occasions for the same reasons. He may dance around a gaily decorated tree, or learn about wassailing, or about gift-giving—these are pre-Christian or pagan in origin and common to many societies. He may be enthralled with Dickens' *Christmas Carol* or other stories about Christmas. But he will not find himself an outsider at a Christmas service. Neither will he fail to distinguish between these cultural trimmings and the essential holiness to Christians of the celebrations that take place in their own homes and churches, where they will find the holy day and worship the Holy Child. He will understand and respect the home and church traditions of others because he has his own events of spiritual-ethical-religious significance in his way of life, which he celebrates at home or in his place of religious gathering. In turn he will enjoy the understanding and respect of others.

35

The Commission can make no prescription. It can only suggest the limitations and point out the spirit within which solutions must be found. It suggests that what is best for a given community, even for an individual school, will not come as a compromise among religious views, nor as a vector from varying pressures. Rather will it come from the careful planning, school by school, of programs that fall within the obvious limits and that reflect the considered concern for the maximum growth of children in a religiously diverse school and society.

In a public school which has regularly found occasions for children to tell about their own and hear about others' religious celebrations, rites, and beliefs, few problems arise. The teacher sets the atmosphere. He or she need only be warmly interested and supportive for children to see that their differing customs and beliefs are neither strange nor the cause for estrangement but are rather wonderful and essential elements of a pluralistic society. The trap for the teacher who has not deliberately thought through his own role lies in his unconscious identification with one of the religions or groupings of religions. How easy it is for a committed Christian to speak of "we" and "our" ways, unconsciously thereby leading children to identify the "we" with the school and government or world, and perhaps themselves with the outcast or minority "they"! It becomes hard for them then to see that the schools and the government do not belong to Congregationalists or Catholics or Baptists or Adventists or Jews or Ethical Culturists or Humanists or Atheists—but to the people as citizens with their citizenship in common, whatever their religious diversities.

There is a vast difference in spirit and effect between a school's "own" Christmas pageant or Christmas displays on the one hand, and an exposition by some children to other children of their family, cultural, and church customs and rites, when it is one of a series of expositions at appropriate times of differing customs and rites designed to build a common appreciation of the many religious contributions to our heritage, on the other hand. The former is establishment of religion, the assertion of "a" school religion. The latter is a recognition of the deep importance to each child of his own religion and to all people of the varying religious commitments of their fellow citizens.

Even if or perhaps especially when a particular school might appear to be made up exclusively of children of one religious affiliation, their citizenship development requires that they learn that other citizens of their community, state, and nation have other affiliations while sharing equally as citizens.

The Commission recommends the policy that encourages reasonable recognition of Christmas in the schools in the spirit of exposition of the differing rites and customs of families, cultures, and creeds—each with deep meaning for its adherents, and in sum revealing the many different religious, philosophical, and cultural practices and beliefs held by Americans.

The public schools are and of a right should be responsive to their communities, within constitutional and other relevant limits. But they also have uniquely the commitment to teach the meaning, the obligations, and the rights of citizenship, including the necessity for protection against the establishment of religion and against intrusion on the religious freedoms of any and all citizens in the United States. In such a context, Christmas in the schools becomes a manageable problem and a potential asset.

B. The School Calendar and Individual Religious Obligations

There is no calendar which perfectly meets all of the different needs for marking the passage of time. However, in most of the more advanced nations of the world there is now a common civil calendar which takes into account the solar and lunar cycles with considerable accuracy. This calendar, the Gregorian, was worked out under the patronage of Pope Gregory XIII and promulgated in 1582. It was adopted in England 170 years later and in the American colonies at the same time. For the first time the seasons fell in the same calendar segments and the equinox was pinned to a very narrow range of days in the fall and spring. This is the calendar used in the civil and business affairs of all "Christian" and many other nations.

Although Pope Gregory established Christmas as December 25th and many of the events of the Christian church year fall on fixed calendar dates in relation to Christmas, neither the Christian church calendar nor that of any other religious group coincides exactly with the civil calendar.

On the Christian church calendar Easter is what is called a movable feast date. For each civil calendar year, the date of Easter is established according to a complex formula which is related to the first full moon after the vernal equinox. The formula is an elaborate one and complicated further by an occasional artificially established equinox date, and by the fact that when the date for Easter would coincide with the first day of Passover it is moved to the following Sunday. Because of these provisions, Easter is observed on a Sunday which falls on the civil calendar on dates which, according to the *Encyclopedia Americana,* range between March 22nd and April 25th.

38

Christian holy days whose dates are related directly to the date of Easter include Ash Wednesday, the fortieth day before Easter; Palm Sunday, the Sunday before Easter; Holy (Maundy) Thursday, the Thursday before Easter; Good Friday, the third day before Easter; Ascension Day, the fortieth day after Easter (a Thursday); and Pentecost (Whitsunday), the fiftieth day (a Sunday) after Easter.

Fixed dates in the several Christian church calendars, many related to Christmas, include the Feast of the Immaculate Conception, December 8; the first Sunday in Advent, the fourth Sunday before Christmas; All Saints Day, November 1; the Feast of the Circumcision, January 1; the Feast of the Epiphany, January 6; and the Feast of the Assumption, August 15. For some Protestant denominations Reformation Day, October 31, is also a significant day.

Sunday has a special legal place in the civil calendar. The Supreme Court has upheld certain Blue Laws on the grounds that basically Sunday has come to be "a day of rest" in the secular world. Because of this, the holy days of the Christian church which fall on Sunday have no effect on the school calendar, except as they may affect out-of-school activities. Christmas and New Year's Day also enjoy a special status as legal holidays. Of the other holy days, with the growing exception of Good Friday and excepting that Saturday is observed as the Sabbath by certain Christian as well as by Jewish denominations, the past practice of the churches has been to schedule religious observances and obligations in such a way as to require no interruption to the normal working or school day. In some localities more recently, a few churches have scheduled children's activities on certain holy days at times that conflict with the school day.

The Jewish calendar is not directly related to the civil calendar. It received its present fixed form from Hillel II in about 360 A.D. Although most holy days fall on a date which is fixed on the Jewish calendar, there are a few which shift slightly to make a harmonious arrangement.

The most striking fact about the Jewish calendar is that there is a periodic addition of one whole month to bring the year back into relationship with the solar and lunar cycles every 19 years. This puts the Jewish New Year (Rosh Hashanah) on a civil calendar date that, according to a table in the *Jewish Encyclopedia,* ranges between September 6 and October 5, and affects other holy days accordingly.

Webster's New International Dictionary lists 10 holidays observed in Judaism, most of which include more than one day. The B'nai B'rith Memo and Date Book (a valuable desk calendar with a glossary of holidays, available through that organization) lists and describes these:

> *In the Jewish tradition, the day lasts from sunset to sunset; thus the Jewish Sabbath and all other Jewish holidays begin [at sunset] on the evening preceding the day of observance. Major Jewish festivals include Rosh Hashanah, Yom Kippur, Pesach, Shevuoth, and Sukkoth. On these holidays, Jewish children may be absent from school depending on synagogue and home requirements and practices.*

In the observance of Jewish holy days, as distinct from Christian holy days other than Sunday at least, it should be noticed that the observance requires the person's presence at home or in his synagogue for much longer periods; in effect one either gives the whole day to the observance or does not observe it.

Other religions use other calendars, although the Orthodox Church calendar is similar to the Gregorian calendar.

The public school calendar varies from state to state and

40

even from district to district within the state. It is usually governed by some fundamental legislative requirement for the number of days school is to be in session, as well as by other statutes which require the schools to observe special days, some by closing. In contrast to a calendar of working days in the business and industrial world, the typical public school calendar is established not so much by specifying the holidays as it is by designing a schedule of days on which school shall be in session that will meet the state requirements for the number of school days and will be compatible with the civil and, in some cases, church calendars.

Most public school calendars, including calendars of out-of-school activities, are almost entirely shaped to the Christian holy days. Besides the legally established holidays, many public schools do not now operate on Good Friday, for example. A small but increasing number of school districts have also tried to take into account the church calendars of other groups significantly represented in the district, although adaptation to the Jewish church calendar is made difficult by the wide range of movement of the holy days and the varying versions of Judaism.

Some school districts have tried to make provision for at least the first day of Rosh Hashanah, a two-day festival; Yom Kippur; and occasionally the first day of Sukkoth, which is an eight-day festival—all of which regularly fall in or near September. In addition they often take into account the first day of Pesach (Passover), an eight-day festival which always falls very close to the Christian Easter. Less often they will recognize the first day of Shevuoth, which usually comes in June.

Since setting the annual school calendar is ordinarily a duty delegated and detailed in part by the state legislatures, the Commission here only calls attention to the problem. It urges that in the development of a district's school calendar every effort should be made to give support to the freest possible exercise of religious obligations by the children and staff.

In some years the school calendar might easily take into account both the significant Christian holy days and the most important Jewish holy days. In 1964-65, for example, Rosh Hashanah falls on Labor Day and the day following; Yom Kippur falls on Wednesday, September 16th; Pesach starts on the day before Easter and closes on the following Saturday; and Shevuoth falls on Sunday and Monday, June 6th and 7th.

The Commission recommends that the policies under which school calendars are established be such as to guarantee to the maximum the possibility of appropriate religious observances by all children and staff members, while providing at least the legal requirement for number of full days in uninterrupted session for the school itself.

C. Absences for Religious Observance

Personnel policies need examination. To the extent that the school calendar for teachers and employees makes demands that conflict with their religious obligations, special provisions are necessary. In practice these provisions vary greatly.

There are some districts in which Jewish teachers, for example, are not excused and in effect are prevented from observing their High Holy Days. Only a little less restrictive are other school districts where teacher absence for such purposes is permitted but only at the loss of salary.

Another arrangement is found in some school districts

42

which permit absence for religious observance but charge that absence against the paid leave for sickness.

The Commission recommends that where the school calendar involves a conflict for people of some or any religious faiths, provision be made in school districts for staff absence without undue penalty for necessary individual religious observance. It notes that in a few districts with this sort of provision, such absence is charged against a fixed allowance for absences for "cogent personal reasons." Since there is a delicate Constitutional question involved, prudence dictates that form of allowance to lessen the possibility of the invoking of the establishment clause.

Where the school calendar does not take into account all of the principal days of religious obligation for its students, the Commission recommends that with appropriate safeguards children be freely excused on such days and that as a matter of policy no school examinations or other highly important school activity be scheduled for those days.

The nature and degree of the problem obviously varies tremendously from district to district and even from school to school within the district. There are school districts in which all children, to the extent that they participate in their religious observances, are in the same cluster of denominations. There are schools where on a Jewish holiday many or most of the teachers are out for observance, and very few of the children are out. The reverse is also true. But whatever the circumstance in a given district at a given time, the Commission recommends that policies affecting the school calendar, personnel practices, and children's religious observances be surveyed periodically to ensure that they neither penalize nor make difficult religious observances by any or all of the people under the school's jurisdiction.

43

D. Cooperation in After-School and Out-of-School Activities

Public school educators recognize that school is only one of many agencies and forces in the educational development of the children it serves. Sound policy requires that the schools seek actively to adapt their after-school activities and out-of-school requirements to minimize conflict in children's time and interest with such church-connected activities as late afternoon religious classes, youth programs, and other obligations and opportunities provided by the churches to children outside of the formal school day and week.

Many unnecessary conflicts are avoided when communications are kept open and flowing between those who are responsible for such church-connected programs and the public school administrators. At one extreme there is the case where an all-school concert was scheduled for the very afternoon of an interfaith rally. This seems inexcusable. Such a conflict for children's loyalty and time could take place only when there was substantially no communication between the schools and the churches.

In these days when pressures for out-of-school study in connection with the school program are mounting and when the so-called extracurricular activities are flourishing, it may be impossible to avoid conflict completely. However, some districts are finding ways to minimize the competition for children's out-of-school time.

Some of the same consideration must be given to the members of the staff so that they may fulfill their own religious obligations and their families', and may continue, as is so frequently the case, to teach or otherwise serve their own religious institution's programs for children and youth.

44

The line between cooperation and establishment is difficult to draw. With respect to the so-called released time programs, there are fairly clear legal guides. Historically such programs have ebbed and flowed. At their peak they enrolled only a very small fraction of the total number of public school students. The two Supreme Court decisions in this matter, along with some carefully drawn state statutes and regulations, provide guidance for such practice as is found today. The legality of released time seems to hinge pretty largely on the showing that no public resources are used and no element of coercion is present.

The Commission discovered practices in some school districts which represent a most extreme form of cooperation with groups of churches. In one county it was reported that "the superintendents of the school systems in the entire county have been actively interested in the work of the Sunday School Council." The schools grant and record school credit for attendance at Sunday School. Teachers are required to make reports, record credits, and send periodic reports to the school offices, and from them to the superintendents' offices. School resources and school support are used to encourage youngsters to attend their several Sunday Schools (including at least one Saturday School for Jewish children).

This practice is highly unusual and is subject to challenge. Since such a challenge is outside the intended scope of this report, the Commission only urges all districts to examine objectively all their forms of cooperation against the dual obligation to promote the free exercise of religion by appropriate cooperation with other agencies in the development of children, and punctiliously to avoid any semblance of religious establishment by using public resources or even subtle coercion.

45

One practice which the Commission endorses, subject only to Constitutional interpretation, is the setting aside of a bulletin board in the school building on which community organizations may display notices of meetings of interest to segments of the school's population including their church youth activities, all under appropriate safeguards.

E. Staff Composition

One of the ways of ensuring good communication and mutual understanding in the community is to have a faculty and staff who themselves represent diverse religious faiths and affiliations. Unfortunately it is common in communities of a changing complexity to find the distribution of religious affiliations within the staff becoming quite unrepresentative of the total community population. ‹This is a matter of great delicacy and sensitive good sense. Religious discrimination in staff recruitment is forbidden in many states and probably under the Constitution. But if a staff is made up exclusively of people of the same or closely related religious backgrounds, it is evidence of one kind of religious discrimination, however unintended. If the public schools profess to teach the positive inherent values of a pluralistic society, they are all the more bound to practice those values. One way is to reflect a religious pluralism within the school's staff.

In the building of a staff the first consideration is competence, of course. But there is an analogy with school boards. A school board which is composed by conscious selection of one woman, one Catholic, one Jew, one Presbyterian, one banker, and one farmer, for example, is hardly more desirable than one which is only representative of a prevailing power structure. So it is with school staff. The Scylla of a staff all with the same religious background is at least as potentially bad as the Charybdis of one that is handpicked and minutely balanced to conform to some predetermined pattern, even a pattern of religious diversity. The productive and fair course lies somewhere between.

Too, school administrators are accustomed to dealing with problems of balance in a school staff. They often are looking for some sort of balance between men and women, balance in the geographical backgrounds, and balance in the special interests and potential contributions that elementary teachers have to make in science, music, art, and the like. Here the Commission urges only that an effective staff is one which is at least as diverse in its religious background as are the children in the schools. It could be argued that the diversity should be greater, in order to open the eyes and extend the horizons of the children. Such considerations in practice and in law must of course take second place to the overruling criterion of competence.

F. High School Baccalaureates

There are a number of practices and customs with religious overtones in which tradition varies sharply among school districts and among the states, and for which little specific guidance has so far been provided in Supreme Court interpretations or other legal sources. In this category fall the widespread use of high school baccalaureate services, of dedications and cornerstone layings, and of invocations at ceremonial occasions.

The baccalaureate service was borrowed directly from collegiate tradition. Many high schools and even some lower schools have adopted the custom as part of the graduation ceremonies. Although there may be some question as to the suitability of a program "of or pertaining to a bachelor's degree" for high school graduation, the more sensitive point is the avowedly religious nature of the service itself.

In school districts where some kind of baccalaureate is included as part of the graduation process it is handled in one of five ways:

1. Where there is a single dominant religious denomination, the service is often traditionally conducted in the school auditorium by the clergyman of that denomination. In these conditions the degree of denominationalism of the content will vary according to the sensitivity of the pastor. But strictly sectarian or not, it is basically a church service in a public school, and students are in effect required to participate. It would seem rather clearly to fall under the prohibitions of the First Amendment.

2. In some high schools clergymen from more than one denomination participate in a given baccalaureate, or the selection is rotated annually among some or all of the local clergymen. Implicitly, this arrangement frankly recognizes the religious and denominational nature of the service. Where the clergymen rotate the theory is that over a period of time the school's graduates will have been exposed to a number of different religions, although in practice each graduate will have had only one such exposure. This is a religious service, subject to challenge as such.

3. In other districts baccalaureate services are held under school auspices in a local church, or in annual rotation among churches that can and will provide the facility. The chief difference from custom just cited lies in the fact that the service is conducted outside of the school building itself. For both this and the preceding custom, the Constitutional question may hinge on whether the school requires its students to attend a religious service under school auspices, either within

the school itself or in a local church or churches. The degree of compulsion or sponsorship and the reasons for the service —its "purpose and effect"—are factors which would seem to be critical in testing the constitutionality of these practices.

4. A few districts have sought to meet the Constitutional issue by continuing the baccalaureate service but stripping it of all directly religious content. They substitute inspirational poetry and prose for Bible reading and prayer, and a general exhortation for the baccalaureate sermon. The issue here is not one of form or of substance. Rather it is a matter of context. Because the baccalaureate is traditionally religious, the substitute service becomes, by the fact of substitution, open to question as an "establishment" of Humanism as an official religion.

5. The fifth solution is for religious groups represented by students in the graduating class to conduct baccalaureate services in their own churches and synagogues. In communities where some of the churches are accustomed to unite for special services a number of them may join in a union service for their own graduates. In others, every church will hold its own. In any case, the school does not require attendance nor does it do more than inform its seniors about this opportunity as it might about any other church-sponsored youth activity.

The Commission recommends this fifth practice as being compatible with sound Constitutional and educational policy. The school administrator, by taking personal initiative in the matter, in one step recognizes the important role of the churches in the lives of their own young people, avoids imposing any single religious point of view on a captive audience, and yet actively suggests the importance of high school graduation as a still momentous step in the young person's development.

G. Dedications

Dedication ceremonies are quite a different matter. A public school building represents the results of the hard work and the culmination of the selfless dreams of a good many fine people both within and outside the school staffs. It is the creation of people through their government and their taxes. It is natural for those who are most immediately concerned to breathe a prayer of thankfulness, and for all to wish to set the building apart with due ceremony for a special use. To those in the Judaeo-Christian tradition, such lines as "Except the Lord build the house, they labour in vain that build it," come to mind. To others these particular words may be unfamiliar, yet some comparable sentiment wells up from within their own tradition.

There are some who feel that it is inappropriate to dedicate in any religious terms a building which is essentially secular. They reason that the public tax dollar came from people and property with many and no religious labels, and they propose that good manners would prevent the arrogation of all good motives and noble aspirations to any single religion or group of religions.

Some of the difficulty may be eliminated by noting just what it means to "dedicate" a school. *Webster's New International Dictionary,* second edition, gives five definitions for the verb *dedicate:*

1. To devote exclusively to the service or worship of a divine being; or to sacred uses; to set apart with solemn rites . . .
2. To set apart formally or seriously to a definite use, end, or service . . .
3. To inscribe, address, or name by way of compliment, honor, or the like . . .
4. To open or present to the public formally . . . (Colloq.)

5. (Law) To give or surrender by way of dedication (sense 2).

Definitions 2 and 4 are clearly applicable, and number 3 may be. Formalities are a cherished part of community life. Those who hold high the value of public education look on the dedication ceremonial as a way of recognizing the community's response to its civic obligation, and of honoring those whose leadership and labor have culminated in the concrete embodiment of the community's aspirations. These are worthy reasons for a dedication ceremony.

At the same time the young people who are to use the new building will profit from a ceremonious recognition of the community support not only for the building itself but also for the educational opportunities it makes possible. Altogether, there is much to be said for a formal dedication, particularly if it is consciously planned to give emphasis both to past accomplishment and future obligation.

One solution which recognizes the religious pluralism of a community is an open and honestly meant invitation to all citizens or groups of citizens to come together at a given time, each to make a dedication according to its appropriate rites and customs.

Another way, which has sound educational value, is to encourage the students to conduct a dedication ceremony which recognizes those who made the new building possible and pledges that those who use the building will do their best to justify that faith.

The Commission recommends a dedication ceremony that both recognizes and sets apart formally to a definite service—a ceremony conducted in a spirit of accommodation and good taste, and particularly one that makes students aware of the trust and confidence the community has so concretely displayed in its contribution.

51

H. Invocations

The matter of invocations and prayer at these and other ceremonials and occasions are practices in which the most careful reading of the decisions and dicta of the Supreme Court presents a confused picture.

American people have commonly experienced the courtesy of standing quietly in the presence of one whose religious manner, phrasing, and habits of prayer may be quite alien to some. To adults in a religiously pluralistic society it does not seem to be bothersome. Problems arise when the person praying seems to be an official representative for the rest in a religious matter.

On great state occasions, illustrated by the President's Inauguration, several religious leaders have often participated. Through that variety has been mirrored the much greater diversity among the citizenry. Similarly in public school occasions the inclusion of religious leaders of several different sects may be used to represent even great diversity.

It should be noted that the public schools are in a peculiarly sensitive position because of the proper concern of parents and churches for their children's religious development and freedom from any element of coercion in behalf of a different religion.

This is an area in which true freedoms will develop slowly. It is one in which, excepting for classroom prayers, little controversy has yet arisen. So far at least, the Supreme Court has made a distinction between ceremonial occasions and the regular incorporation of school prayer.

The Commission recommends that such consideration as good manners, good taste, and a concern for the sensitivities and an awareness of the diversity of the faiths and affiliations of those present will dictate the wise course.

52

I. Multiple Religious Observances

Finally, among the practices discovered by the Commission is one found occasionally in schools which involve their children in a succession of religious observances of the holy days of a variety of sects. For example a public school with substantial Jewish membership may add an observance of Hanukah in a mistaken effort to "balance off" the Christmas pageant. It seems clear that if one religious observance is forbidden then two or more are no better. The Commission set out under its discussion of Christmas its best judgment on more appropriate ways to build understanding and respect in all children for the religious customs and beliefs of others.

J. Conclusion

The Commission has taken up in turn each of many common school policies and practices on which the basic American Constitutional ideals of freedom of religion, freedom for religion, and freedom from governmental establishment of religion seem to have some bearing. In each case, the Commission has sought to locate the sensitive points and recommend only those policies and practices which in its best judgment are consistent both with educational ideals and Constitutional limitations, along with a recognition that the last word has not yet been said nor the final wisdom yet achieved.

V

THE CURRICULUM AND
OUR RELIGIOUS HERITAGE

---

*Nearly everything in our culture worth transmitting,
everything which gives meaning to life, is saturated with
the religious influences derived from paganism, Judaism,
Christianity—both Catholic and Protestant—and other
faiths accepted by a large part of the world's peoples.*

THE PUBLIC SCHOOLS have as one of their principal roles
the transmission of culture, the passing on of the rich heritage
of the American people. Justice Jackson, in the quotation
from the *McCollum* case which heads this chapter, reminds
us of the significant part religions have played in that cultural
heritage. The Commission believes that the public school
curriculum must give suitable attention to the religious influences in man's development.

54

A curriculum which ignored religion would itself have serious religious implications. It would seem to proclaim that religion has not been as real in men's lives as health or politics or economics. By omission it would appear to deny that religion has been and is important in man's history—a denial of the obvious. In day-by-day practice, the topic can not be avoided. As an integral part of man's culture, it must be included.

Whatever else the Supreme Court decisions may or may not have done, they have stimulated the public schools to a search for appropriate means to deal effectively with religion as one of the great influences in man's history. Some school districts, state agencies, and educational groups have renewed their efforts to develop materials that will strengthen and enrich the curriculum in these respects. Some teacher preparation institutions are earnestly at work trying to define their obligations and to derive and test programs that are educationally sound, objective, and consistent with both the constitutional and educational requirements of the public schools.

The task is challenging. No perfect answers have been found. But the Commission believes that better and more appropriate materials and methods will be developed as the nature of the challenge is more widely understood, and as educators themselves move to meet it. The answers are not to be expected from those who either do not understand or do not accept the distinction between teaching *about* religion and teaching *for* religion, between examining religion as a cultural phenomenon and indoctrinating in a religion. Neither will they come from those who, misreading the requirement of neutralism, eliminate all references to religion or seem to substitute a nontheist humanism. The constructive contributions will be made by those who are sensitive to the delicacy and intricacy of the task; who can combine the contributions of the wisest students of the humanities with those of the most knowledgeable students of teaching and learning; who can call upon the ablest public school teachers; and who have the courage and resources to provide for continuous objective evaluation and appropriate revision. This is a big order, but one infinitely worth the effort.

The Commission recognizes three distinct policy areas, related to each other and to the subject of this report, where explicit educational policy, adequate materials, and effective methods need to be developed. In one large area, recognition must be given to the role of religion and the religious in literature, in history and the humanities, and in the arts. In a second area ways must be found to portray the part played by religion in establishing and maintaining the moral and ethical values that the school seeks to develop and transmit. Finally, the public schools are called on to build an understanding of the relationships between civil government and religious freedom, and to prepare youth for citizenship in a multifaithed society.

A. Religion in the Cultural Heritage

The King James version of the Bible, the New England Primer, and the Horn Book were the basic educational and literary tools for generations of early Americans, along with the works of Shakespeare, who himself was nurtured on an earlier version of the Bible and whose writings are filled with Biblical language and imagery. These books, often the only library in early homes and settlements, furnished much of the common core in the development of early American culture, particularly among the English settlers.

America's cultural heritage is a complex one and it would be oversimplification to emphasize its English origins exclusively. Other cultures made major, distinctive contributions. As for religious foundations, the separate early colonies, some founded as refuges from religious persecution, were themselves often religiously exclusive. They made no place for people who would not accept the established religion. This built some homogeneity within the particular colony but does not account for the evolving community of the colonies. That growth rested on common experiences, shared dangers, and the growing interweaving of interests. No small strand in the growing ties was the common culture in which common literature and common educational tools played a prominent part.

Back of the national heritage is the whole development of Western civilization itself. Its history cannot be understood without some understanding of the great religious and church influences reaching back to the earliest of recorded times. From the beginning, a sizeable share of the art, drama, music, and literature in this heritage from the past was grounded in and reflects Biblical and church influences.

In a recent book, *Teacher Education and Religion,* referred to in more detail later, Kenneth S. Cooper, professor of history at George Peabody College for Teachers, says that "knowledge about religion is an important aspect of the scholarly study of society." This view is complemented in the same volume by Knox C. Hill, associate professor of humanities at the University of Chicago, who said that the study of humanities should "extend the capacity for positive sympathy —not merely negative tolerance—for the expressions of religious literature and art."

These expressions are quoted with approval. The Commission is aware of the great difficulties in the way both of developing detailed syllabuses and of ensuring that teachers

57

are prepared to deal with such topics effectively and fairly. It commends to all individuals and agencies concerned the most scrupulous efforts to meet these difficulties.

The study of comparative religion and the history of religion are parts of the graduate programs in theological schools and are taught as courses in many colleges. The objectivity and maturity required seem to make such studies inappropriate in elementary schools because of the age of the students. At the secondary level judgment on the appropriateness can not be justified until more evidence is available.

Some question may be raised as to whether high school students have yet reached the necessary maturity for such studies. Further, there is little evidence that teachers in the secondary schools are fully equipped and qualified to teach such courses. Most inhibiting to the development of effective programs is the scarcity of suitable material in usable form.

The answer to the question of student maturity will come only after well-prepared teachers with skillfully designed materials have had an opportunity to try to teach these topics and the outcomes can be soundly evaluated. As for teacher qualifications, in-service opportunities to develop competence have already been demonstrated to be effective in other areas of the curriculum and might easily be provided here. But the real rub comes in the meagerness of the material available that is truly objective, balanced, and educationally sound.

There is a good deal of local improvisation of materials. There are some state-wide efforts. But what is needed is a heavily supported project led by educators, calling on scholars in the humanities and in the religions, and using the best programming and presentation skills available. The medium in which the material is developed might well be a series of short sound films, usable in individual classrooms or for wider broadcast, but the form it takes is incidental to the vision, competence, and understanding of those who produce it. There are precedents for this kind of scholar-teacher production, notably in the sciences.

The Commission strongly favors the production of material of the highest educational and technical excellence in the history of religion and comparative religion. It supports strongly the prudence that would put direction of the project in the hands of public school educators who are intimately aware of the possibilities and limitations under which the materials may be used. It asserts that such a project requires access to resources beyond the reach of a local school district or of most state departments of public instruction. Finally the Commission believes that the objectives to be sought are so appealing and necessary as to make it possible to attract financial support from sources outside of either governmental or denominational agencies.

In the more familiar fields of the public school curriculum—music, art, literature, history, and the social studies— the problems are at the same time more simple and more complex. In the social studies, for example, it seems simple to suggest that what is required is the development of a religious literacy comparable to the economic, political, ethnological, psychological, and sociological literacy already posed as desirable outcomes. In fact, objectivity and broad understanding are comparably difficult for the teacher to achieve and for the materials to embody. The answer is not easy. In great part it rests on the kind of preparation teachers (and textbook and syllabus writers) have had for their tasks, and on an environment which values justice and objectivity.

The report referred to earlier—*Teacher Education and Religion* by a commission of the American Association of Colleges of Teacher Education (published in Washington in 1959)—represents the continuing efforts of institutions

59

preparing teachers to discover ways to develop the competence needed to deal wisely with these problems. The Commission commends this evidence of the institutions' concern. It urges all institutions of higher education in their teacher education programs to give careful thought and appropriate attention to the need for developing the competence required of teachers in these fields.

Teachers of music and art and, to some degree, of literature, often seem to have been better equipped with an appreciation of the contributions of religion in their fields. The history of these arts, usually a required study for teachers, is a history of values and of man's view of himself, his world, and his God or gods. Much of the classical work in all the arts is deeply indebted to and affected by the religion and the religious institutions of the time. True literacy in the arts almost inescapably involves a degree of religious literacy. Art history, survey and criticism, or what are commonly called "appreciation" courses, would be empty without some understanding and appreciation of the religious element.

The desirable policy in the schools, as the Commission sees it, is to deal directly and objectively with religion whenever and wherever it is intrinsic to learning experience in the various fields of study, and to seek out appropriate ways to teach what has been aptly called "the reciprocal relation" between religion and the other elements in' human culture. The implementation of that policy calls for much more than an added course, either for teachers or for the high school curriculum itself. It requires topic-by-topic analysis of the separate courses, and cooperative efforts by the teachers to give appropriate attention to these relationships.

Without seeming to pass all problems back to institutions preparing teachers, the Commission still would urge that they undertake the kind of investigations, experimentation, and alteration in teacher education that is properly in their province. In the meanwhile the working profession can profitably use all the familiar proven devices by which curricular and instructional improvements are commonly made.

B. Values

For more than a century every major attempt to set out the objectives of public education has included high in the list one or more statements about the development of character or of values. Many books, reports, anthologies, and syllabuses have been published on the subject or as guides to its teaching.

Latterly there has grown up a body of research in the development of values. The findings raise serious questions about some of the long-held assumptions about the effectiveness of many of our educational programs, curriculums, and institutions in their influence on the value systems of students. Much of the public reaction to recent Supreme Court decisions seems to some to reflect more alarm about the possible impact on children's values than concern about their religious ignorance. Research and reaction together make value development a subject of current concern and debate—as it has been since the first recorded discussions of education and child rearing.

In this connection the Commission once more quotes with approval from *Teacher Education and Religion* the position reported in the summary chapter, which would have the school teach "the part which organized religion has played in establishing the moral and ethical values that schools must develop and transmit. Giving due respect to the principle of valuing differences in a free society, it would not

61

seek to equate religion and morality by suggesting that religious convictions or sanctions alone undergird moral principles or ethical imperatives. It would, however, acknowledge the resources found by most people in religion as a basis for durable convictions and moral and ethical imperatives."

Educators have long been concerned with defining and implementing the public schools' own ethical imperatives. Their commitment to the processes and goals of education has led them to a sound distaste for "indoctrination." At the same time there is a nearly universal consensus that the schools have an important part to play in the building of character and in the development and reinforcement of value systems that are consonant with the values commonly expressed (though perhaps less commonly embodied) in the larger society. Few dispute the wisdom, even the sheer necessity for personal fulfillment, of every individual's commitment to something higher than self and more than the passing moment.

The public schools themselves represent a commitment by the American people, part of a larger commitment to "establish justice, insure domestic tranquillity, provide for the common defence, promote the general welfare, and secure the blessings of liberty to ourselves and our posterity," in the words of our Constitution's Preamble. Every public officer, in the states as in the nation, has taken an oath to support the Constitution. There seems to be no educational or ethical reason why every citizen, young or old, should not be led toward the same commitment.

There are other moral and ethical values, not in every case sanctioned so explicitly, but common to most or all of the world's religions and philosophies. They rest on a sort of universal wisdom about the relationships to others and the controls over self that make men truly free, that fire each man to find for his brothers as for himself the highest fulfillment.

Commitments, or values, are both taught and caught. They are everlastingly expressed and implied in the child's environment—in school and out. They literally permeate the public school. In the schools the element, held by some to be critical, that is missing—and must be kept so—is the ultimate sanction of religion as devotion or creed. The element that by any view is vital is a recognition, by all who organize the school environment and confront the child in person or indirectly, that values inevitably are being embodied and hence, in a real sense, taught.

The Commission believes that sound public and educational policy requires of our public schools that in all they are they shall embody, and in all they do they shall help develop, worthy moral and ethical values. Such a policy becomes a bill of rights and responsibilities for all, from the board of education through all segments of the staff to the children themselves.

C. Preparing for Citizenship in a Multifaithed Society

The early reactions to the latest Supreme Court decisions call attention to another pressing need. Far too few appeared to understand that primarily the Bill of Rights is a great bulwark designed to protect the individual from the state. Too many seemed to have overlooked or failed to attend to Justice Jackson, speaking for the Court in *West Virginia Board of Education v. Barnette* (1943):

> *The very purpose of a Bill of Rights was to withdraw certain subjects from the vicissitudes of political controversy, to place them beyond the reach of majorities and officials. . . . One's right to freedom of worship . . . and*

63

other fundamental rights may not be submitted to vote;
they depend on the outcome of no elections.

Few apparently heard or heeded Justice Clark's words in the last paragraph of the Court's opinion in the *Schempp* case (1963):

The place of religion in our society is an exalted one, achieved through a long tradition of reliance on the home, the church and the inviolable citadel of the individual heart and mind. We have come to recognize through bitter experience that it is not within the power of government to invade that citadel, whether its purpose or effect be to aid or oppose, to advance or retard. In the relationship between man and religion, the State is firmly committed to a position of neutrality.

The widespread first reaction points to a real need. Surely every public school child must learn what is expressed and implied in the great compact, the Constitution of the United States of America, which undergirds our national society. He must know the history of the Bill of Rights and what it means. In the subject of this report, specifically, the First Amendment's guarantees in the field of religion must be widely comprehended. Students need to know what Lord Acton meant when he said that there is no greater tyranny than a democracy without restraint. Only as all citizens know and understand the issues which caused our founding fathers to insist on the inclusion of the Bill of Rights as a condition to the adoption of the Constitution can they come to intelligent and informed judgment.

There are other possible constitutional compacts. The Constitution itself provides orderly means for its own alteration. But before advocating or supporting change in its terms the prudent citizen will first learn the background and reasoning that produced the Bill of Rights. Then he will study hard and think long and objectively about the probable long consequences of alternative national Constitutional positions. He will not amend lightly the compact that has served the nation so constantly for a century and three quarters.

If and when the public schools have achieved their assigned role in the education of America's citizens, they will justify Samuel Johnson's dictum that "about things on which the public thinks *long* it commonly attains to think right." The real issue will be clear. At stake is not what the Constitution means in its present form, but whether it or some other policy or compact will best guarantee to all citizens a true religious freedom.

This issue needs to be seen in perspective. In the centuries since the separate colonies began to come together, the cultural heritage has become even more complex and varied. Yet it is possible to speak of an American heritage, an American dream, an American way of life. Among the elements at the heart of this heritage are the freedoms guaranteed in the First Amendment—freedom from establishment of religion and freedom of religion.

The challenge to the public schools continues to lie, in large part, in the development of free men for a free society. The Commission urges that building understanding and support for the Bill of Rights with their attendant obligations is a requirement on the public schools, to be reflected in policy and practice.

D. Conclusion

Throughout its report the Commission has recognized the unassailable fact that America is a pluralistic society. High on the list of diversities that make our nation strong is the diversity among public school districts and the communities they serve.

The Commission has not tried to prescribe or propose a policy or set of policies for all districts. It has pointed to needs and suggested approaches to meeting them. Above all, it has sought to call attention to the obligation on every school district and on every state to establish constructive policy in the many fields in which religion touches upon the operation and curriculum of our public schools.

America's public schools have a long, rich, and unique history. They are founded on a singular view of the good society. They cherish differences. They respect individuality. They reflect and build an order in which differences—religious and ideological as well as natural—are regarded as contributing strength not weakness. The common faith they nourish is a faith in freedom, the matching of right with responsibility.

The power of the public school is in the opportunity it provides for the creative engagement of differences—differences in physical and mental capacities and characteristics, differences in background and culture, differences in the creeds men live by. This is a power not always understood, not uniformly supported, nor invariably exercised effectively. Concern over the role of religion in the public school that leads to a lessening of that power weakens the very institution that serves a diverse society so faithfully. Concern that leads to improvement in the methods, materials, and competence with which the school deals with the role of religion is constructive. The Commission has earnestly tried to respond to this latter concern.

The challenge is immense. It can not be met fully by any district alone or immediately by all in concert. Yet the Commission is confident that America's public schools can

66

and will find ways to meet that challenge, to preserve the guarantees of religious freedom while reinforcing for each the free exercise of his religion, in a society which gives full respect to those of every faith and creed.